ISBN-13: 978-1453755334
ISBN-10: 1453755330

To learn more about Nahid, please visit www.Mehjati.com

I AM SINAI

Who Said Autistic Children Cannot Learn?

My Family

Author: Nahid Mehjati (Azimirad)

Illustrator: Mina Tavakoli

I Dedicate This Book . . .

To my great mom Goli, my daughter Arshnoosh, my son Arash, and my husband Hassan for their endless love and support which are nourishing my dreams to come true.

I acknowledge Niza, Sinai's mother, for her enthusiasm, constant encouragement and cooperation.

I would like to express my gratitude to Shirin Tavakoli for editing the lexical semantic aspects of this book.

Who is Sinai?

Sinai is an autistic girl who was non-verbal during her pre-kindergarten years. The incredible impact of the booklets on Sinai and other autistic children, as well as the children's remarkable progress, inspired the author to publish this book.

Sinai, like many other ASD (Autistic Spectrum Disorder) children, has talents which have neither been identified nor have reached their full potential development level.

Please look for other themes in the

I AM SINAI: Who Said Autistic Children Cannot Learn?

book series

My name is Sinai.

I am a girl.

This is my home.

This is my family.

This is my Daddy.

This is my Mommy.

I have two brothers.

This is my older brother.
He goes to college.

This is my younger brother. We both go to school.

He jumps with me on trampoline.

Daddy goes to work.

Mommy works and studies on computer.

Daddy makes the best
fries for me.

Mommy cleans
the house.

She goes shopping.

Mommy does the laundry.

Mommy cooks
yummy foods.

At home, she plays
with me.

Mommy helps me with
the homework.

I love my family.